SAINT KABIR

His Rustic Wisdom

SAINT KABIR

His Rustic Wisdom

Prof. D.P. Agrawal

PILGRIMS

PILGRIMS PUBLISHING
◆ Varanasi ◆

SAINT KABIR: His Rustic Wisdom

D.P. Agrawal

Published by:
PILGRIMS PUBLISHING

An imprint of:
PILGRIMS BOOK HOUSE
(Distributors in India)
B 27/98 A-8, Nawabganj Road
Durga Kund, Varanasi-221010, India
Tel: 91-542- 2314060, 2312456
E-mail: pilgrims@satyam.net.in
Website: www.pilgrimsbooks.com

Layout by Roohi Burchett
Cover Design by Asha Mishra

ISBN: 81-7769-467-7

Printed in India at Pilgrim Press Pvt. Ltd. Lalpur Varanasi

Foreword

While the world is struggling to improve the quality of human life and avoid conflict, there are parallel forces, which are highly retrograde to achieving lasting peace and harmony in human society. Even developed nations of the world appear to be sick.

> "In nature there is no blemish but the mind"
>
> —Shakespeare

The root cause of suffering is the mentality of the people. The big question is, 'can the sick mentality of people be remedied?' We have been failing in our efforts. But we have to keep trying because we have no alternative. Kabir's rustic wisdom may be tried.

Author

Prof. D.P. Agrawal
'Kabir Jayanti' 2006
98, Shivajinagar,
Varanasi-221010

Saint Kabir: His Rustic Wisdom

India during the 13th century was subjugated by the Muslim Sultanate. It was a period of political anarchy. There were several Hindu suzerainties scattered over different parts of the country and the Muslim Sultanate, which claimed a central authority was weak due to which, indiscipline ruled supreme. The small and scattered pockets of strength were busy serving their vested interest and the country's economy was ruined. The depleted economy resulted in poor production and appalling scarcity.

There was frequent famine. Unemployment was rampant and the majority of people had no resources to buy articles of daily necessity. The rich had grown richer and the poor had become beggars. The life of the common man was miserable. The uneducated and illiterate masses had become slaves to those few who had amassed all the resources for themselves. They had become self-styled guardians of the conscience of their slave people. Religious extremism had become the order of the day. It was the darkest period in the history of India. The Hindu as well as the Muslim priests had thoroughly brainwashed the people to resign themselves to their lot. They were almost forced to accept that their misery was divinely ordained.

The priests had conveniently made the highly religious minded people to own their misery as god's will, and that they were destined to suffer due to their misdeeds in their previous birth. They were almost hypnotized to accept the dogma of destiny. Poor people, Hindus as well as Muslims, both of them were obliged to serve the domineering ecclesiastical powers. Priests and their cronies were enjoying life by exploiting the poor people, using them as commodities. Such unjust social condition prevailed in India when Saint Kabir was born in Lahartara a village in Varanasi district of U.P. State in the year 1440. According to the legend, he was born on 'Kamalvan'(कमलवन)—a thick growth of a hundred thousand lotus flowers in a huge lake of the village. It is said that the lake was so huge that it looked like the river Ganga. The lake was fed by the river, flowing about a mile away. Waves were formed in the waters of the lake because the river water kept regularly pushing into it. That was why it was named 'Lahartal' (लहरताल), meaning a lake of waves. The name of the village 'Lahartara' (लहरतारा) has been derived from the same. Even to day there stands a small ancient temple cum mosque type of structure marking the birthplace of Saint Kabir. There is only a remnant of the lake with very little water in it on the eastern bank of which the small monument stands, perhaps most part of the lake has been filled in and new residential houses along with other structures have come up. However the remnant of the lake and the structure are being taken care of by the Kabir Mutt and the local administration.

From his birthplace the babe was rescued by a couple who adopted him as their son and took him to their house in Narharpura (नरहरपुरा), now known as Kabirchaura in the heart of Varanasi city. Kabir was brought up there by his foster parents who were weavers by profession. They were Muslims but they never performed any ceremony to brand 'Kabir'. Therefore Kabir remained just a human being and a humanitarian all through his life. He neither offered 'Namaz' nor performed any Hindu Pooja (worship), although his parents were Muslim and he accepted a Hindu, named Swami Ramanand, as his teacher. But he never got himself initiated into any religion. He thought out his independent philosophy of life like a theosophist of modern days.

The 'Kabirchaura Mutt' is the head office of Kabir-system. This place is the spot where child Kabir grew under the guardianship of his foster parents. Since they were weavers, Kabir also assisted them in their work. Thus Kabir learnt the art of weaving and by the time he attained adulthood, he was a trained weaver himself. Kabir adopted that profession for himself and earned his living thereby. He was satisfied in whatever small earning he had and he made his work his worship.

Kabir's philosophy of work developed in his mind while weaving cloth, which was his daily routine.

He regularly took sometime off from his work to visit saints and scholars at Varanasi to learn from them about religion. Kabir was an illiterate person. Therefore, he attended the discourses of the scholar priests and often made queries to clarify his doubts. In this manner Kabir educated himself because, being illiterate, he could learn only by listening and questioning. When he gained some knowledge he tried to express his ideas through small verses, which he was fond of composing. Since Kabir, did not know writing, his utterances were noted down by his literate fellow men. It can be appreciated how laborious the entire process must have been.

The Hindu ethos during the period of Saint Kabir consisted of multiple philosophies. One school of thought was Shankaracharya's Vedantic philosophy of (Nirguna) abstract God while the other school was 'Saguna'. There was the school of 'Love' promoted by Chaitanya. The other similar school of thought was 'Sufi'. On one hand there were those sects that were followers of caste-system and on the other there were non-believers in any such classification. Of the casteless sects were Ramanand Rai of Jagannathpuri in Orissa and the 'Salavars' of south India who carried influence of the north, and were opposed to Shankaracharya. Then there was the sect of Saint Gorakhnath who also was opposed to the caste classification. Buddhist philosophy was a casteless and atheistic philosophy, which was under attack by the Brahmin thinking. Islam already had a firm foothold in India by the time 'Kabir' appeared on the scene. The iconoclastic misadventures had prepared ground for religious tussles with the idol-worshippers. In short, there was a cultural upheaval in the Indian society when Saint Kabir intervened by rejecting all parochial thoughts, which were detrimental to social harmony and unity in the society. The Indian society at that time was a cross section of various cultures. There were the Hindus, the Muslims, the Buddhists and so forth. Egalitarianism of the Vedic era was lost under pressure of the Brahmanic philosophy of dividing people on the basis of caste, which had come to be accepted as divinely ordained. The iconoclastic extremism had injured the Hindu ethos, and was hurting their sentiments. Buddhists had become soft target of the lamentably orthodox Brahmanic violence. Society had disintegrated to the farthest limit. A state of chaos prevailed and life of the common man was miserable.

Saint Kabir said, no child is born with a class-tag on him. Every one is born as a human being and he remains so until, after his birth a class tag is put on him by the agents of a particular class. On the basis of that tag the human beings are sorted out into different baskets. This acts as the beginning of disintegration in the society. The agents of the different classes of human beings used the people dropped into their basket to serve their vested interest. These agents were the various priests who carried different brand names and made a business of religion. They pretended to have God locked in their possession for the benefit of the people of their basket. They thoroughly brainwash their people to keep them under subjugation lest they should run away from their trap. For this purpose every priest invented ritualistic paraphernalia to keep their subjects bound under their spell. Kabir, though illiterate, had a sharp mind, and could see the nefarious design of the priests who, acting as experts, drove their people to perform ritualistic paraphernalia and in return collected gifts in cash and kind, from their disciples. Kabir realised the irrationality of such performances, which he derided.

Kabir delivered to the world an egalitarian philosophy of life, in simple words and poetic style, which the common man could sing and enjoy. Six centuries have passed and the common man, the farm worker, the shepherd, the coolie, the man in the street all enjoy singing Kabir's songs, even at their work. The common folk also understand the underlying meaning of Kabir's songs. Even the illiterate derive spiritual pleasure in singing the songs. Kabir sang for the common folk and was himself a commoner. Therefore his literature is folk-literature, created in simple words, which conveys deep spiritual thoughts and touches the heart. On account of these unique qualities, Kabir's literature continues to be popular even today, six centuries after its composition.

Since Kabir was a man of the proletariat, the illiterate and half-educated masses of India could readily identify with him and adopt his views. The unique features of Kabir's literature are: [1] language of the masses [2] lyrical and touching style [3] class and caste-free spiritual thought-content: rustic yet high-minded social philosophy. Almost for a millennium prior to Kabir's birth, Brahmanic order had crushed the working classes who were leading a wretched life of slaves. They were serving the so-called higher classes, other than 'Shudra' (शूद्र). The higher classes had confiscated all the human rights of the 'Shudras', who were serving the higher classes under lurking fear of being exterminated. Kabir himself belonged to the same low class; but he was bold enough to propagate the philosophy of social equality by rejecting all types of separatist classification of human beings. Kabir was a revolutionary and he carried on his mission facing heavy odds. The proletariat, naturally, began flocking around him and he became their hero. However, the opposition to Kabir from the vested interest was so powerful that Kabir could not transform the society, yet he set the ball rolling and his ideal became a beacon for the generations to come. Kabir did not travel far and wide for achieving his mission, and he remained mostly centred in Varanasi, which has been a religious hub of India. Yet his missions today are working in different corners of the world.

There is a jungle of guidance groups and schools of philosophies of life in India, which are currently active. All of them are selling their wares. They are attracting clients by systematic publicity. All of them are vociferous and loud. Obviously their multifarious activities and attractive programmes, which are periodically arranged, seem to be capital intensive. Their devoted followers may be financing their programmes. Some of them, perhaps, are supported by overseas sources. It is good that they are highlighting the concept of spirituality in the modern world, by modern methods of management. As against the prevailing position of the sale of spirituality, the Kabir Mutt is conducting its programme on a low key. Perhaps Kabir Mutt would do well to come out of its shell and spread out a little more in India itself. Perhaps, our own people are not fully informed on the subject. More and better co-ordination of inland activity may be the first priority. However, spreading out of the country is permissible. In fact the Kabir-philosophy has already spread out to foreign lands like Mauritius and Trinidad etc., where there is a concentration of Indian ethnic groups.

Kabir was an exponent of egalitarian views. A classless and casteless society alone is the guarantee of peace and progress in modern day strife and tension. Priority needs to be given to transform his ideas into action. If we introspect we feel lacking in that direction. We have also to assess the degree of our readiness to socialize on the economic front. We have also to ascertain that capitalism provides breathing space to the proletariat, otherwise the present class-war cannot be checked and the society will continue to be sick. Kabir was tired of emphasizing this reality to which the society has been oblivious. He has expressed his agony in the following words:

कबिरा या संसार को समझायो सौ बार।
पूँछ न पकड़ै भेंड़ की उतरा चाहै पार।।

During the medieval period of Indian history the egalitarian value system of the people was completely wrecked. The people were divided into separate groups, which had lost sight of the larger interest of the entire race. Frustration among the majority had overtaken their sentiment, which had lapsed into negativity and social disharmony. Kabir's effort was to heal the wounded psyche of the people and bring back equanimity in the social relationships of the people, and to repair their value system by emphasizing the concept of equality and social justice.

Kabir communicated with the people in their own dialect, and hence the masses also could understand him easily. His philosophy was to take all people along for everyone's welfare (सर्व–जन हिताय). Orthodox religious orders, both Hindu as well as Muslim, were opposed to him. But Kabir being popular, kept the torch of egalitarianism burning in the face of opposition, which failed for want of popular moral support.

The social revolution which Kabir generated and carried forward during his lifetime, is still continued through his mission's branches. But it lacks the charismatic leadership of Kabir who could inspire the masses to march ahead on the path shown by him. The imperative need of energizing the Kabir mission and its revolution is now being felt. It is to be realised that Kabir's non-violent revolution can be a very healthy alternative to the various terrorist methods of land reforms which are spreading hatred and disharmony among the people.

Divergent methods of the various religions in India during the 15th century were accentuating the disagreement among people of different faiths instead of finding commonality of their purpose. In Prof. Abdul Kalam's view, '...we have learnt to adjust to the rifts and divisions in our society. We must regain our broad outlook and draw upon our heritage and wisdom—our spiritual development.' Much earlier Dr. Annie Besant had said, "The union of religions lies in the spiritual truth in the philosophic ideas and above all in mysticism when man discovers himself as belonging to Him the soul of the universe, and seeks to return to Him whence he came". Hindus say 'So Hum' सोहं *(I am That);* Tat-Tvam-Asi तत्वमसि *(That is Thee);* Sufis say An-al-Haq, Haq-Tu-i *(I am God Thou art God);* Kabir in the languages of the masses says:

कहै कबीर विचार करि, जिन खोजो कोई दूरि।
ध्यान धरौ मन सुद्ध करि, राम रहा भरपूरि।।

(Why go far to find Him. Think of yourself with pure heart, Thou art He.)

Kabir presented philosophy in the language of the masses, making it so simple that even the illiterate could understand. Kabir himself was illiterate and he knew no other language than that of the masses—the multitude of illiterate people of our land. In order that they could sing it and remember it better, Kabir put his ideas in short verses in simple words. This is a unique feature of Kabir's presentation, as also of other saints of that age, like Tulsi who sang in the language of the masses, and not in Sanskrit of which he was a master. Kabir appears to have given a healing touch to the wounded ethos of the masses by providing them moral and cultural leadership and pulling their spirits out of deadly morass in which it had landed.

With the rise of the ecclesiastical power, rituals acquired precedence over the spiritual concept. The plethora of religious paraphernalia eclipsed the intellectual wisdom, and consequently obsession instead of logic, ruined the Vedic ethos of equality. People became class conscious and the united and firm Vedic fabric of the society drifted apart and weakened. Caste hierarchy was formed and the so-called higher class reserved all the privileges for themselves at the cost of their weaker and underprivileged brethren. History witnessed the fact that after the collapse of the Vedic society whenever dissatisfaction in the deprived majority of the people increased, revolt against the prevalent system precipitated, resulting in violence in the society. The oppressive social situation always throws up a leader—a deliverer. Krishna was one Buddha was another.

Under exactly similar condition Saint Kabir came in our midst to assuage the feelings of the masses. His message was for humanism, which rejected classification of people either by caste or by faith. The multitude of deprived and confused people, subdued under the spell of the self styled agents of divinity, the charlatans of ritualistic magic, revolted against the oppression and gloom which loomed large in the life of the so called lower classes. Kabir rejected all dogmatic ideas prevalent in the different sections of the society, and put the Hindu priest as well as the Muslim mullah in the dock. They opposed Kabir with all their might but were unsuccessful in their attempts because the weaker people, suffering long under their patronage had become thoroughly disillusioned. A revolt had precipitated which found moral support under the charismatic leadership of Saint Kabir.

Kabir's revolt against religious orthodoxy was not an upsurge. It was a moral revolution against dogmatic thinking, against meaningless ritualistic paraphernalia to extract money from the ignorant, though devoted masses. It was a revolt against the organised blackmail of the innocent people, and their slavery at the hands of ecclesia. Kabir was the first Indian to raise his voice against exploitation. He was an exponent of egalitarianism, and his philosophy was based on equality and social justice.

Saint Kabir had the realization that the root cause of suffering was misdistribution of resources in the society. Social tension has its origin in unjust sharing of loaves and fishes. Therefore, he advised people not to amass wealth or other resources. He said, people should have only enough to satisfy their need and that of their family members.

साँई इतना दीजिए जामै कुटुम समाय।
मैं भी भूखा ना रहूँ साधु न भूखा जाय॥

Labour (श्रम)

The natural and benevolent human effort or labour was the religion of Kabir, which is frequently mentioned in many of the thousands of verses he uttered and which were collected by his literate disciples. In Kabir's view, concentration of resources in a few hands in the society was the root cause of social tension. In fact when only a few persons in the society will collect all the resources, naturally the majority of the people who work and produce those resources, would suffer deprivation. There will be struggle for the sharing of the resources. Therefore equitable distribution of resources is imperative for social harmony. Scientific analysis of the developed and underdeveloped economies to day, perhaps, confirms Kabir's rustic view regarding distribution of resources among the 'haves and have-nots'. The Indian ethos from time immemorial has been against the concentration of wealth (अपरिग्रह). Kabir reiterated the same by highlighting it, as people were losing sight of that egalitarian principle due to selfishness and greed.

Saint Kabir set a unique example of living up to the ideal he preached. He belonged to the working class of people. His father Neeru, was a weaver. Kabir adopted the same profession for himself and earned his living thereby. He never accepted any gift nor did he ever beg for his bread. He earned it by working like any other weaver, weaving cloth. He lived with his family like any other worker in India. Work was his worship. When a person works with his hand, with total devotion to the item of his work, his mental concentration lifts his consciousness from the mundane to the higher and higher levels of spirituality, and to the ultimate level—to the very root from whence his personal consciousness originates.

The prevalent exoteric religions during Kabir's period consisted of innumerable rituals and obsessive practices, shorn of logic and simplicity. Kabir's penetrating intelligence and spiritual inclination did not find any meaning in those exoteric practices. Therefore he rejected all types of rituals, and also ridiculed them, whether Hindu or Muslim.

"पाहन पूजे हरि मिलै तो मैं पूजूँ पहार,
घर की चकिया कोई न पूजै जेहिका पीसा खाय"।
"कांकर पाथर जोरि करि मस्जिद लई चुनाय,
तेहि चढ़ि मुल्ला बाँग दे बहिरा हुआ खुदाय"।

Manual labour is the foundation of Kabir's model of religion. Since Kabir was a labourer himself, work was worship for him; and his weaving loom was his God. When he put all his heart and soul into his work, perhaps the pace of his heart synchronised with the pace of his loom and from that he could connect his work with his heart beat. He then perceived the connection between body and soul and at a still higher level of integration between his personal soul and the universal soul. In that sublime state of mental integration he could visualise the relationship between the 'Atman' (आत्मन्) and 'Paramatman' (परमात्मन्). This was not only his science but also his art of making relationship between 'work' and 'worship' to discover God. Therefore 'work' is the core concept of Kabir's system, which may be better termed 'Yoga' —the Kabir way.

This concept of the relationship between Yoga and work has a social relevance; and it is the corner stone of Kabir's philosophy. Kabir's period was a feudal period in India. Manual labour had come to be rated low in the scale of social values. Kabir tried to glorify 'labour', which Gandhi also did much later. It is to the credit of mass-leaders like them for visualising the far reaching implication of labour oriented policies for equanimity in the society. This was also conducive to quality production and cost-effective too. In a country like India where teeming millions of paupers (दरिद्रनारायण) are to be looked after by the society, only a labour oriented economy can maintain harmony and which should go a long way to build a strong nation. As such, Kabir's concept of work-based worship is relevant even today.

Equality (समता)

The next point, which is the basis of Kabir's philosophy, is the concept of the equality of all human beings. He rejected all types of classifications of people, particularly those that were conducive to disturb equanimity in the society. He was totally against caste classification.

> एक त्वचा, हाड़ मल मूता एक रूधिर एक गूदा,
> एक बूँद से सृष्टि रची है को बाभन को सूदा।
> वहि माटी की गागर होती, सो भर के मैं आणी,
> सो मिट्टी के हम तुम दोनों, छूत कहाँ लिपटाणी।।

Society was divided not only on the basis of caste but also on economic levels. A small minority of rich people had reserved most of the facilities for themselves and the majority of people were left with no option but to live on scanty resources, ill clothed and half-fed. Exploitation of people thrived on the basis of unjust classification of people. The advantaged class was insensitive to the miserable condition of the deprived classes who had no alternative but to meekly accept their depravity as divinely ordained. The dogma of destiny, propagated by the self styled guardians of the society, and the ecclesiastic, had thoroughly brainwashed the people to suffer their plight as an irrevocable destiny. Such condition continued for about a thousand years when orthodox Brahmanism had acquired great authority and also patronage of the kings. Prior to Kabir's time, the mysticism, dogma of divinely ordained systems and unshakable adherence to the obsession of destiny had overtaken the better part human reasoning. People had been suffering under the spell of mass hypnotism, created by the ecclesiastical power. Kabir found his fellow contemporaries leading a wretched life silently, yet not having courage to rebel against the unjust order.

The common man's morale was low and they had resigned themselves to their bad luck, taking it to be God's will. The rationale of accepting their suffering as their destiny was fixated in their minds because that was the mental mechanism which the advantaged class of Brahmins had cleverly invented to gain total control of the masses. Therefore, people had completely surrendered to the ecclesia without questioning the rationality of their injunctions. In the state of such deplorable plight of the people the prime need was to rescue their psyche from the systematic indoctrination, which had been the priests' instrument to grill them for centuries. Kabir's revolutionary fervour waged a frontal attack on the system of priesthood, by openly rejecting every dogma they preached. Kabir's move was conducive to making a big dent on priesthood and also in boosting the morale of the downtrodden.

'... मानुषा मानुषानेव दास भावेन भुञ्जते।' Enslaving human beings was never approved in human history, and yet it is a fact that enslaving human beings was prevalent in ancient societies everywhere. The above-mentioned quotation has been taken from the epic 'Mahabharat'. The context is a dialogue between Rishi Jajali and an ordinary grocer named 'Tuladhar'. When Jajali passed the final exam at his school (Gurukul), his teacher asked Jajali to go back home and take care of his old parents who were weak in health. Hearing this Jajali replied that he would instead go to the forest and meditate about God, which is the highest and noblest 'Dharma'. Upon this Jajali's teacher bade him to go to 'Tuladhar' in order to have better understanding of 'Dharma'. Jajali acted accordingly and approached Tuladhar to have better understanding of 'Dharma'. It was a prolonged dialogue between the two from which the above-mentioned portion has been taken. Tuladhar asks Jalali, 'Is it 'Dharma' that human beings themselves are using other human beings as commodities by enslaving them?' Exploitation of human beings is not 'Dharma', which Kabir also disapproved in no uncertain terms of exploitation. 'Human freedom' is the central feature of Kabir's philosophy, which is nursed by four factors: (1) Equality (समता), (2) Labour (श्रम), (3) Service (सेवा). (4) Love (प्रेम).

Each one of these is equally important. All these four factors together form Kabir's-philosophy. None is primary and no one factor is secondary. Equality is the very basis of the dignity of labour. Kabir himself was a workman, a weaver. He never suspended his weaving work for preaching doctrine. Instead, he discovered spiritual reality while concentrating at his work with undivided and continuous attention. In working with all his mind and heart, Kabir experienced spiritual fulfilment.

Kabir's philosophy of work surpasses Marxism on account of the metaphysical meaning Kabir attaches to work. Kabir's revolutionary fervour emerged from poverty whose most natural resultant was work for earning some money to manage his daily bread. For the hungry food is above everything else in his mind; nobody will give him food unless he worked to earn food. Kabir did not land up in the following situation. "A young man of strong body, weakened by hunger, sat on the walkers portion of the street begging and repeating the sad song of his defeat in life, while suffering from hunger and from humiliation. ...Then he lifted his puzzled eyes to heaven, while hunger was eating his inside, and he said, 'oh Lord...In desperation I asked for alms, but thy worshippers saw me and said, 'He is strong and lazy and he should not beg'.

> "Oh Lord it is thy will that my
> mother gave birth to me, and
> now earth offers me back to
> you before the Ending."
>
> —Khalil Gibran (Tears and Laughter).

While Khalil Gibran's young man felt defeated in life, Kabir never let his spirits down because he worked hard and earned his bread by the sweat of his brow. Therefore 'work' came to occupy the central position in his thoughts, and the basis of his spirituality. His weaving loom became the Lord for him, and, naturally, the act of weaving became worship. That is how work became the foundation of Kabir's spiritual thinking. Kabir's strong will power and his great self-confidence always kept his spirits high. Kabir was a winner. On account of his extraordinary self-confidence, Kabir's philosophy of work became the fountainhead of his revolutionary movement.

The 15th century was a period of feudal oppression in India. Society was divided in two groups of people, (1) the feudal oppressors and (2) the oppressed, the working class of people like agricultural labour, artisans and the service rendering persons including slaves. The second class of people led a wretched life and survived at the mercy of the oppressors. Kabir belonged to the lower classes, who were all workers. Therefore Kabir could appreciate the importance of 'Shram' (labour). He observed that even those people, who did not put in any labour, were dependent on the work performed by others. As such, the realisation came to him that it was only 'Shram' (श्रम) i.e. labour through which human life could sustain. Consequently Kabir attached great importance to the factor of labour (श्रम) in his philosophy. This is also evident from the fact that in his verses, to express his ideas vividly to the common man, Kabir used symbols like the grinding wheel, the weaving loom, the spinning wheel, the water pot, the cooking vessel and such other familiar gadgets from the world of work. Kabir derived strength from the creative power of labour (श्रम). No factor other than positive labour can create and also sustain. Therefore the very survival of human beings depends on that single factor, and hence it is holy. Every person has to participate in this holy performance and one who does not share this duty is a parasite. From this rationale evolve the concept of equality, which is another important centre-point of Kabir philosophy.

Perhaps the principle of equality (समता) is as much an important element of Kabir's philosophy, as labour

(श्रम). Egalitarianism is the ancient Aryan concept, quite familiar to the Indians. But with the rise of ecclesiastical control in India as well as Europe around 15th century, the concept of equality was put on the back burner. Papal power in Europe and its counterpart in India i.e. Brahmanism, had come to acquire undisputed power over the people. As centuries passed under the despotic mandates of the ecclesia, people felt stifled; as a reaction, Martin Luther revolted in the west and Kabir in India. The European rebel being violent and the ecclesiastical power in Europe being ruthless, Martin Luther was put to death, whereas Kabir in India, did not meet the

same fate, though he too suffered untold Brahmanic humiliation and atrocities.

During Kabir's time, i.e. 15th century, the Indian society was divided into a number of sections. Brahmanism had drawn lines between different groups of people within the same ethnic class, and had passed a religions decree in their own favour, acquiring the highest pedestal for themselves. They had proclaimed the classification to be divinely ordained and irrevocable. Thus they had enslaved majority of the people who were bound to offer all sorts of services and also funds to the Brahmins. Vested interest was being shamelessly served by the so-called higher classes whilst the service rendering people were denied the social privileges being enjoyed by the classes, which the Brahmins had declared higher. Such an unjust social order naturally resulted in dissatisfaction among the working class and the service rendering people. Kabir vehemently raised his voice against this system, and blamed the priests for the injustice being meted out to the class, which was declared the lowest (शूद्र). Kabir was a social reformer and a saintly person. He had not only realised but had himself suffered the injustice being done to the people who served the higher classes in the society.

A dividing line already existed between the two major religious groups in India—The Hindus and the Muslims. The division of population on the basis of castes and also their religion frequently resulted in riots, arson and loot. Life of the common man remained disturbed because of the differences between the competing ethnic groups. But the people did not suffer so much due to ethnic riots as due to exploitation by feudal lords and priests who oppressed the financially and socially weaker people.

Naturally, Kabir criticised the affluent people and priests for enjoying the inhuman luxury of using slaves as commodities. Consequently Kabir had to suffer humiliation and threat from the priests who were after his blood. But he never compromised his stand. He braved all the threats aimed at him and plethora of humiliation heaped on him continuously throughout his life at Varanasi. However, Kabir never wavered from his stand on equality, human brotherhood and secularism.

गहना एक कनक तें गहना सा में भाव न दूजा।
कहन सुनन को दुइ करि शाये, एक नमाज एक पूजा।।

(They may look different but all ornaments are gold. Namaz and Pooja may look different but both are prayers).

Saint Kabir had realised that it was imperative to accept the unity of mankind in order to avoid conflict and to maintain peace and harmony in the society. He was dead against priesthood of all religions, because Kabir observed that a priest whether Hindu or Muslim tries to impose upon his client his own doctrine, which he meticulously fashions with meaningless rituals shrouded in impressive paraphernalia and which at times looks mystic to the client. By so doing the priest traps his client into a precarious situation where he gets easily spell bound. And then the priest proceeds to extract pecuniary and other benefits from the client. Kabir disapproved of such nefarious practices of the priests and rejected them altogether.

The frame of reference in Kabir's thinking is the larger unit i.e. humanity. To him individual was certainly important but not with a brand name of religion or a caste-tag. The only brand name of any individual should be humanity. Kabir categorically rejected any classification of human beings, as such.

एक चाम हाड़ मल मूता एक रूधिर एक गूदा।
एक बीज तें सृष्टि रची है को बाभन को सूदा।।

(Skin, bones, blood and all the body is the same. All human beings grow from the same seed: where is the question of Brahmin and 'Shudra' being different).

Kabir struggled to awaken the society which had gone to sleep under the hypnotic spell of different religious healers—the Hindu priests and the Muslim Mullahs. Throughout his life Kabir worked to awaken the society so as to bring back the lost egalitarianism, where there was no prejudice or discrimination between man and man.

During the 'Mahabharat' era also the unity of society was damaged. Social distances between groups had increased. Various clans and ethnic groups had emerged. Negative Social interaction had enlarged the aggressive limits. That unhealthy situation ultimately precipitated the battle of 'Mahabharat'. Appallingly large numbers of precious human lives were lost. In the negatively charged social condition of that age Krishna delivered the message of equality. He succeeded in bringing back peace and order. During Kabir's age too similar abnormal conditions had developed. In the negative social circumstances of his time Kabir also gave the message of equality to the people; but the people's response to his call was weak. Therefore Kabir's success was not spectacular. But undoubtedly Kabir's thoughts on the concept of social equality, and the imperative need for the same for harmony in the society was highly called for. Kabir's thinking is in line with Krishna's consciousness about the subject. The ideas of different social reformers on the concept of equality are similar; and each one of them has held social equality to be the prerequisite for stability in the social structure. Peace can never be had unless we bring about equality in the society.

Service (सेवा)

The third factor in Kabir's social philosophy is service of the people. Service presupposes selflessness. The service rendered for some personal gain or return is not the concept of service. Helping the weak selflessly is real service. Kabir did the same by fighting for the rights of the weakest section of the society i.e., the 'Shudra' (शूद्र). He spoke aloud against the tyranny that was perpetrated by the Brahmin i.e., the highest class of people among the Hindus, and against the exploitation by the Mullah among the Muslims. By being vociferous and loud against all types of exploitation, Kabir built up the self-confidence of the downtrodden and gave them moral strength. Thus he enabled them to speak up and demand their rights.

Kabir has repeatedly expressed his great faith in action and not in religion. Feeding the hungry, comforting the sick, protecting the helpless, lightening other's burden and to gladden the hearts of others are acts of service.

ओरों को हँसते देखो मनु, हँसो और सुख पाओ।
अपने सुख को विस्तृत कर लो, सबको सुखी बनाओ।।

—— महाकवि 'प्रसाद'

Gladden others' hearts to gladden your heart, share others' joys and extend your joy to all.

Real service is the service to human beings rendered selflessly. It is like charity, which is doubly blessed. It blesses the taker and the giver alike, it relieves the recipient and unburdens the heart of the donor. This is the third pillar of Kabir's philosophy.

Love :

Love is the fourth ingredient of Kabir's philosophy. Kabir, as a babe, was rescued by his foster parents who brought him up out of sheer love and compassion. Love is the food for the soul.

प्रेम न बाड़ी नीपजै, प्रेम न हाट बिकाय,
राजा रंक फकीर सबै सीस देइ लै जाय।

(Love is not vegetable which is grown in the garden or sold in the market. Anyone, irrespective of his class, can have it by giving up his ego).

Love is free from ego. It emanates from an ego less state. A person with a big ego is condemned to hell like Satan. Therefore humility is the prerequisite of 'Love'. It is the delicate-most emotion of mankind. It is also the most benevolent and doubly blessed. It blesses both—the giver as well as the receiver. Kabir has laid great emphasis on this factor. Kabir's period was a period of 'Love of God' (भक्तिकाल) in India, and perhaps all Kabir's contemporary poet-saints *('Tulsi', 'Meera', 'Soora')* have based their entire literary work on the 'Love of God'. In fact love of God is also love of His creation in which human beings occupy the highest position.

" ढाई आखर प्रेम का, पढ़ै सो पंडित होय "

(One who has learnt two and half letters of the word 'love' is really learned.)

The above-mentioned verse of Kabir amply highlights the emphasis he laid on the factor of 'Love'.

Kabir's philosophy was a philosophy of work (कर्म) and also a concept of love (प्रेम). The 'love' that was a philosophy was not for individual but for the people, the society. Love for an individual is based on the motive of personal gain; there is duality and not unity in the relationship of personal gain. In true love nothing is personal. Unity is the law of love. All dualities dissolve in the emotion of love. The highest pleasure comes in the service of the better part of the self and the better part of all the selves is one and the same the invisible one, i.e. the Unity. When Kabir talks of love, he does not talk of the mundane, he talks of the spiritual love which unites mankind. True love unites and thereby dissolves the duality. All religions teach love and compassion. The role of religion should be not to let it remain limited to one's own faith, but to make it universal.

उदार चरितानां तु वसुधैव कुटुम्बकम् ।
(For the compassionate, world is the family)

The Bible says, "Love thy neighbour". Rabia, a lady, mentioned by Ibn Khalikan (1211-1282 A.D.), goes to the house-top at night and says, Oh, God, hushed is the day's noise; with his beloved is the lover, I have Thee for my Lover, and alone with Thee I enjoy." Kabir instructed people to love and not to hate, because love unites whereas hatred divides. God is one, His names may be different :

"सहस्रनाम्ने पुरूषाय शाश्वते (The names of that Eternal Being are a thousand)". Therefore, Kabir said, there should be no dispute over names, and no quarrel over His worship, which may be done in a thousand ways. What is important, is compassion and mutual understanding and love. Mutual acceptance is the foundation of love and hence, mutual respect and acceptance has to be promoted so that it may generate love.

To sum up, we may say that there is no mysticism in Kabir's philosophy of life. If is very realistic and is related to the weaker section of the society. It is based on the reality of life of the down trodden who were suppressed by the affluent consisting of the Brahmans and other so called higher classes. Kabir based his judgement on actual observation of people's life during his time. In fact, much of the same was the result of his first hand experience. It goes without saying that Kabir's thinking represented the thinking of the proletariat to which Kabir himself belonged. Kabir was more a worker than a dreamer, although he did talk of the 'Atman' (आत्मा) and the 'Parmatman' (परमात्मन). Kabir's thoughts were practical and down to earth; and hence he laid great emphasis on the economy. Moreover his philosophy was labour oriented and therefore he emphasised, firstly the factor of production of wealth i.e. 'Labour' (श्रम), and secondly equitable distribution of resources. Kabir's philosophy had its origin in the psyche of a developing people i.e., the Indians. The same also may offer some insight to the present day world, in tackling the problem of 'haves and have-nots'.

+